Victorian Chic

Victorian Chic

Anita Louise Crane

Sterling Publishing Co., Inc. New York

A Sterling/Chapelle Book

CHAPELLE LTD.

Owner: Editor:
Jo Packham Kristi Torsak

Staff:
Areta Bingham • Kass Burchett • Marilyn Goff •
Holly Hollingsworth • Susan Jorgensen •
Kimberly Maw • Barbara Milburn • Linda Orton •
Karmen Quinney • Leslie Ridenour • Cindy Stoeckl •
Gina Swapp • Kim Taylor • Sara Toliver

Photographer: Photo Stylist:
Scot Zimmerman Anita Louise Crane

Library of Congress Cataloging-in-Publication Data Available
Crane, Anita Louise
    Victorian Chic
        p.cm.
    "A Sterling/Chapelle book."
    Includes index
    ISBN 0-8069-7495-8 Hardcover
    ISBN 1-402-0128-4 Paperback
    1. Victoriana in interior decoration 2. Decoration and ornament--
Victorian style. I. Title

NK2115.5V53 C73 2001
747.2'048--dc21   2001020116

10 9 8 7 6 5 4 3 2 1

First paperback edition published in 2002 by
Sterling Publishing Company, Inc.,
387 Park Avenue South, New York, NY 10016
© 2001 by Anita Louise Crane
Distributed in Canada by Sterling Publishing
℅ Canadian Manda Group, One Atlantic Avenue,
Suite 105 Toronto, Ontario, Canada M6K 3E7
Distributed in Australia by Capricorn Link (Australia) Pty Ltd.
P.O. Box 704, Windsor, NSW 2756, Australia
Printed in China
All Rights Reserved
Sterling ISBN 0-8069-7495-8 Hardcover
        ISBN 1-4027-0128-4 Paperback

If you have any questions or comments, please contact:

Chapelle Ltd., Inc.,
P. O. Box 9252
Ogden, UT 84409
(801) 621-2777
FAX (801) 621-2788
e-mail: Chapelle@chapelleltd.com
website: www.chapelleltd.com

A Special Thanks

This book is dedicated to Kim Freeman and Nancy Lindemeyer at Victoria Magazine for their inspiration of the timeless grace, charm, and nurturing spirit of the Victorian life-style.
Thank you for enriching my life.

I would like to thank my friend, Dixie Barber, for allowing us to photograph her lovely home. I would also like to thank Dixie for the wonderful food that she prepared for the photographs.

I would like to thank Suzanne Gray and Kathy Pace for welcoming us into their homes to photograph; and thank you to the owners of the Norfolk Cottage in Park City, Utah, for letting us transform their vacation home into a "Summer Cottage."

I would also like to thank my editor, Kristi Torsak, for her excellent contribution and attention to detail. Kristi has not only made this book beautiful to look at, but a very helpful guide to achieving a very Victorian look.

I would also like to thank Scot Zimmerman for the wonderful photographs.

A very special thank you to Jo Packham for editing and contributing to the text. I could not have completed this book without the dedication and hard work of the wonderful staff at Chapelle, thank you.

Last, but not least, to my husband Bruce, for living in a home that is constantly changing.

Anita Louise Crane

We would like to offer our sincere appreciation for the valuable support given in the creation of this book by the following businesses:

Pfaff Sewing Machines
610 Winters Ave.
Paramus, NJ 07653
1-201-262-7211
www.pfaff-us-cda.com

Calico Corners
6150 S. State St.
Murray, UT 84107
1-800-213-6366
www.calicocorners.com

Hip and Humble
2030 S. 900 E.
Salt Lake City, UT 84105
1-801-467-3130

Karastan Carpets
P.O. Box 12069
Calhoun, GA 30703
1-800-234-1120
www.karastan.com

Sugar House Antiques
2120 S. Highland Dr.
Salt Lake City, UT 84106
1-801-487-5084

Designer Textiles
974 E. 2100 S. Ste. C
Salt Lake City, UT 84106
1-801-466-4000

Faye Foster Antiques
4 Central Sq. Unit 2
Bristol, NH 03243
1-603-744-9130

About the Author

Anita Louise Crane is the loving mother of four, and grandmother of nine. She lives with her husband Bruce and her kitty Raisen in Park City, Utah. She spends much of her time on her unlimited talents. Anita enjoys hiking, cross-country skiing, and snowshoeing in the beautiful Wasatch Mountain Range. She has been doing what most people only dream of doing since 1981. It was then that she decided to focus her energy on her true passions: designing, photographing, painting, and writing. Since then, she has developed her "hobbies" into a notable career of making adorable teddy bears, exceptionally beautiful bridal gowns, and attractive paintings and illustrations.

As a distinguished decorator and photo stylist, Anita has also authored many books—*Teddy Bear Magic, Two-Hour Teddy Bears, Two-Hour Dolls' Clothes, Making Adorable Teddy Bears, Adorable Furniture for Dolls and Teddy Bears, Two-Hour Scrap Crafts, and Decorating with Seashells.* Anita is currently writing and illustrating her first children's book.

The once proprietress of the Bearlace Cottage in Park City, Utah, Anita used her design talents and chic style to bring the community her unique teddy bears and elegant gowns. Anita collects antique laces and linens and in the past, sewed timeless bridal gowns from her own lovely and original designs. She is best known for her individually designed and fashioned teddy bears. Her handsome bears are created with love and care. In everything, her style reflects romantic Victorian charm. She now runs her Bearlace Cottage business from her home by appointment. You can learn more by visiting www.bearlace.com.

Table of Contents

Foreword

The romantic, vintage, shabby-chic style of the Victorian period is a gathering of luxurious things, some given as gifts that are delicate and feminine, some collected from nature, and some that are beautifully worn acquired antiques. It was a time for collecting pretty odds and ends, combining beloved old pieces with favorite new finds, and appreciating the lovelier objects of a gentler time that surrounded both the humble and the noble.

As Anita has decorated her own home in this Victorian style, she has recreated the soul of the Victorian period. She has refashioned the dilapidated elegance of homes that contained pieces which were useful, well loved, and comfortable. She is a collector of many things. Few are rare or costly, the majority of which she has found at garage sales, purchased at flea markets, or discovered sitting in the attics of family and friends. She has salvaged many weathered treasures by transforming them into something new and by using what was already at hand in a different place, in a different manner. What is most important to her is the mood that each exquisite detail helps to create. After all, her goal while designing or decorating is always a home that she as well as friends and family all feel wonderfully comfortable in, a home that her loved ones desire to return to often.

Anita is one of those unusually talented artisans that can make something truly lovely out of nothing at all and do it easily; but above all, she is a sweet inspiration to all who know her. She is that which most of us aspire to be.

Living Spaces

Every house where love abides, and friendship is a guest,
is surely home—and home, sweet home—for there the heart can rest.
—*Henry Van Dyke*

How does one begin to make a haven of what now is just a house? Start with an empty space, or a spartan room with furnishings that merely serve their purpose. Then make a sanctuary by surrounding yourself with all of the wonderful things that are loved. Heirloom treasures, gathered collectibles, gifts from beloved friends, and flea-market finds, combined with an abundance of flowers and laces can create a luxurious and comforting retreat from the outside world.

Follow the whim of your hand and the voice of your heart to create rooms that are not only comforting, but reflect your own style and personality. Search everywhere for some lovely trinket or treasure. Learn to love finding unusual ways to use ordinary items and put familiar keepsakes together in fresh and unexpected ways.

A vintage bedspread can become a tablecloth. A graceful window valance was once a lace table runner. A worn, salvaged table is dressed up for tea with layers of linens and laces. Pictures are shuffled, books and boxes are stacked, and blankets are folded and layered. Sofas get new slipcovers, chairs different pillows, and fresh cut flowers are tucked into anything that will hold water. Small trinkets and newly bought china look charming beside old antiques and beloved family heirlooms. Follow your heart and create cozy, inviting rooms furnished with romance and splendor.

Let your imagination take you to your own peace-filled and sentimental sanctuary. In this way, home will become a place where cares can be left at the door, where life is romanced by the things that soothe the soul.

Where does one begin to create such a wonderful place as this? A traditional Victorian-style sitting room where guests are greeted with an easy warm welcome. A place for quiet talks and intimate gatherings among friends. A room of comfort, with cozy sitting arrangements that encourage long, intimate conversations. A place where sunshine spills through light-catching lace and ample cushions invite you to linger among the people and things that are loved.

13

Begin with cherished mementos to surround yourself and guests. This weathered grand pine cupboard is delightful with the graceful formality of the china teapots and pitchers it so proudly displays. Pieces of beautiful lace drape softly over the edges of the shelves. The dark stained, rectangular woven box was the perfect contradiction. Set the serving trays on their sides so delicate hand-painted designs can be seen easily; these create a backdrop for the collected pieces of china. The candelabra with its hanging crystals is a favored piece in this collection. Perhaps, it once brightened a reading nook or end table.

Quilted matelassé coverlets were reborn as soft and comfy pillows to plump up this couch that was slipcovered in a tea-dyed print. Just for a change, the antique oil paintings were hung on the wall without any frames, and flowers from the garden were placed in a tall china pitcher.

A treasured teapot, broken, but rescued from the trash with the help of shells gathered from the sea, accents any shelf or tabletop wonderfully. Carefully chosen seashells that would accent the traditional shape were glued into place. It is no longer completely functional, but something much treasured just the same.

In this sitting room the windows are poetry in white—they are an expression of love and a gentleness of spirit. The use of lace is a way of expressing something of luxury yet simplicity, elegance yet practicality, and that which is delicate yet enduring.

To let in the morning light and the soft shadows of the late afternoon, this main window was draped with a luxuriously fringed coverlet and a valance of gauzy lace was added.

A tiny side window offers much needed privacy with a table runner that is new but casts a delicate shadow on the room.

Few things inspire one more than unexpected details. It is this that takes the ordinary of everyday to the extraordinary of only special days.

A delicate, turn-of-the-century parasol with its rich garden print may remind you of quiet strolls through a sunlit garden. It is one in a collection that is precious—but not rare. It is meant to be lived with and used on sunny afternoons; it was not meant to be put on a shelf left untouched, and unused.

A small much worn table salvaged from extinction becomes a quaint coffee table in this home, dressed in a white lace doily and topped off with a few cherished collectibles—a wooden box, candleholder, and flower vase. A floral, lace-trimmed footstool slips easily underneath. These pieces are part of the effortless living that has come to be known as the "shabby chic" style. Cozy, not fussy, with an appreciation for what is well loved and useful even though it is tattered and worn.

This cozy and quiet corner was created especially for curling up with a romantic novel—happily surrounded by many books and cherished treasures. This great cushy chair with a vintage quilt is a place to snuggle up to read or drift off for an afternoon nap. This sitting area can be changed as easily and quickly as the turning of the seasons. One day it may be surrounded by tall vases filled with flowers from the garden, another day there may be a recently purchased painting and pillows that tempt you to linger for awhile.

When the color palette of a room is as soft and muted as this one, the brighter unframed floral painting becomes a brilliant and lavish bouquet among clouds of lace and dreamy pastels, and the deep rich tones of the oriental carpet are now a jeweled path beneath the feet.

The illusion continues to the whitewashed fireplace along the far wall. In reality, it is only the salvaged mantle of a fireplace from a house long since gone. It has been painted the color of the wall and the frames behind it are flanked with two vintage lamps. Together they provide brilliance and warmth without the firelight. A bouquet of floral fabrics, an outdoor touch of wicker, and an abundance of airy lace were gathered to make the room feel like the extension of an English garden.

Fly home quickly everyday;
We miss you when you're away.
—Anonymous

Each and every new purchase can be added to, embellished, or adorned to make it more beautiful. The lamp on the left is layered with handmade lace squares gently stitched around the shade. Any type of lace or gauzy material will do. For the cardboard boxes stacked to the right, small squared slipcovers were made to hide those things that are necessary and not usually treasured. Because there is rarely enough room for every collected item, one may take to stacking, piling, and layering. In these photographs, layers and stacks of treasures, trinkets, fruit, and flowers grace the tables with their vintage white cloths. The small plaid, beaded heart was originally a Christmas ornament that was simply too charming to box away for another year. These tables are layered with linens and lace, books, embellished boxes, and tiny pillows with buttons and trimmings—and of course, fresh flowers anywhere they will fit!

A quaint bookcase and mirror seem to be a matching set when, actually, the mirror was found years after the bookcases were made.

Here, a stool has been moved from under a coffee table for use as a tiny table to serve afternoon tea.

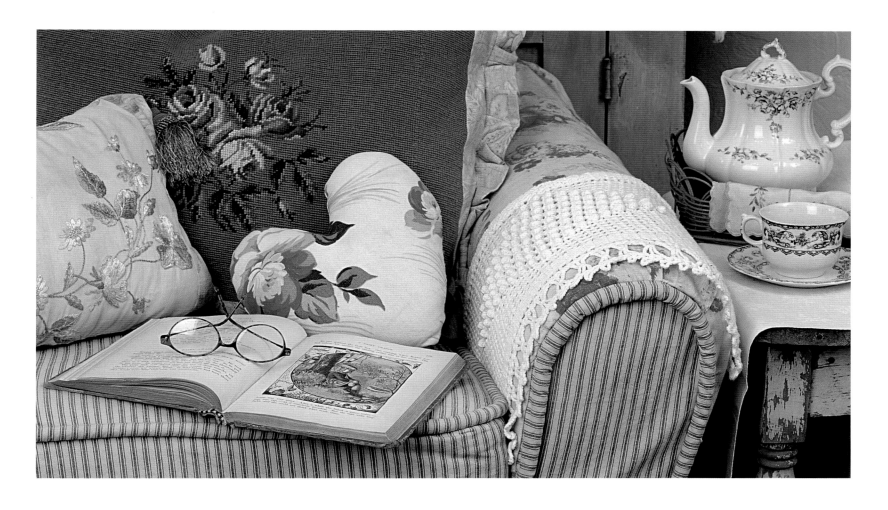

Every old and much loved home should have a sitting room, and this one is occupied by the owner and her cat. It matters not whether she is sitting by the fireplace, sipping a cup of freshly brewed herbal tea and reading, or in a chair, watching out this lace-covered window in the early mornings of fall. This is one place of truth and beauty and no definitive sense of time.

The style here is not as lacy as some homes, but the vintage bamboo mirror, gentle lace window coverings, and Tiffany-style lamps are just as romantic as any Victorian-style home. A collection of antique bottles which have been covered in wicker and gathered together on this mantle may not be traditional Victorian style, but add to the charm of this room just the same.

It seems that those who love to "collect something" love to collect anything and everything. One might begin by buying one or two and then, from that point on, look for one item more to add to the collection. It can be this way with teapots. A collection may have many—all different, yet the same somehow. Most are old, a few are new, some are as if they had never been used, and some show the signs of continued service. It matters not, all can be loved and treasured; and they are even more cherished when used again and again and not stored quietly away for a "special" day.

To justify so many different collections, the collector must find more than a traditional use for those items so lovingly collected. With the teapots for example—they can be used for their original purpose, or they can be used as vases for the flowers from a garden. They can be used as any piece of art, alone or grouped on a tabletop. They can be filled with water for watering plants, or at other times they can hold a potpourri mixture that simmers upon the stove. They can even be used to hold brushes for painting, or a collection of buttons for sewing. There can be as many uses as there are different pots in a collection, some practical, and others simply decorative.

Other important collections to many Victorian enthusiasts are laces and linens. One can have so many as to lose count and often forget about a few if they are tucked in a box somewhere. They can be used frequently; sometimes in their original size and sometimes cut smaller to make pillows or doilies. Some are pleated like a vintage petticoat, some can be as white as winter snow, and some are simple and starched like linens of old. Again, it matters not that they be in mint condition, for those that were much loved and used often are just as beautiful when placed lovingly for all to see.

Not only can you move and rearrange the treasures in a sitting room from shelf to shelf and table to table, you also can change the slipcovers of sofas and chairs with the coming of each new season or with the dawn of each new era in decorating.

Spring might find floral chintz or faded cottons on this chair, but in fall it is most likely to be draped in rich dark fabrics. Once you have made one slipcover the remainder are fairly easy, and they can be quite the alterna- tive to an expensive piece of furniture when fabulous fab- rics are found on closeout. Slipcovers make shopping for furniture a simpler task and one that is not so costly. What you need to look for is not a fabric that is ornate in detail, or one that is the essence of homespun luxury; you need only find a chair that is sturdy, yet comfortable, and has the shape and the lines that you adore. This chair has a western print—a design not fitting in a Victorian-style home—but the rest was exactly what was necessary for this space.

Celestial harmony, warmth, and plenty;
May all this and more adorn your home.
—Anonymous

This chair is wicker and one that can be found in a garden during the months of summer. In the winter, however, it can sit by a window covered with a pretty, lace-trimmed floral-print slipcover. The panel of lace that falls gently down the back of the chair can be removed and replaced with a coordinating cotton print or simply nothing at all. It is attached with tiny snaps under the row of lace. The bow can also be removed, replaced, or left for another day.

Making fabric lamp shades as a finishing touch will enhance any life-style just a little bit more. The shades can be floral or plaid, plain or overdone. They can be trimmed with lace, strung with beads and shells, or have a clean bound edge. They can be dark to let only the hint of light shine through, or light in color and weight so they can be used to read by. Whatever you choose, they are one of many finishing touches.

Summer Cottage

Build thee more stately mansions, O my soul,
As the swift seasons roll! Leave thy low-vaulted past!
—Oliver Wendell Holmes

Your next excursion may be to a quaint cottage filled with sunshine near the ocean, or a holiday in a rustic alpine cabin surrounded by drifts of white snow and the scent of pine. Perhaps business demands a weekend in an uncomfortable hotel room. No matter where your travels take you, or how long you'll be gone, it is easy to pack along beloved treasures that bring friendly remembrances of home, to make anyplace you find yourself more familiar and cozy.

Tote along a mini library of favorite cherished books. Pack sturdy pitchers and vases for flowers, and wherever you are, your first jaunt may be to find a local florist so you can fill the room with fresh blossoms. Arrange things on the tables and shelves just as you would at home—trinkets, bears, and most importantly, pictures of family and loved ones so you may always feel near to them. To happily fill any empty hours, bring a journal along or any supplies for a hobby or craft that you may be working on.

Even a vacation rental can be transformed with your own personal touches, such as squares of laces and linens to layer on the tables and chairs. The familiar pillows and comfy, snug blankets will ease you into sweet slumber and pleasant dreams, as will the friendly ticking of your own bedside clock, even though the bed may be foreign. Tuck sachets of a favorite fragrance into drawers and closets; and a few scented candles placed around the area will add warmth and luminance. Don't forget to save room in your luggage for any treasures you may find to take home.

For some, the sleek rich style of leather and a modern minimalist approach to decorating is practical, comforting, casual, luxurious, and purely simple. It is this with which they choose to surround themselves at the end of a long day filled with an overabundance of stimulus.

It is just such a place that you may find yourself on a rainy day far from home, or a romantic weekend just for two. For many, such a haven would have to be temporarily transformed by treasures that are inspired by the past.

A few boxes of lovely linens and pillow shams, favorite books, and fresh flowers will create a softer place that welcomes old friends, coaxes heart-to-heart talks, and enhances long dream-filled naps.

*All great art is the work of the whole living
creature, body and soul, and chiefly of the soul.*
—*John Ruskin*

Whenever traveling "far" from home, you may want to take three manageable boxes filled with that which you love. The first box can be overflowing with elegant lace coverlets and pillows. Some can be gently placed upon chairs, couches, footstools, and tables. Those that are very sheer and lightly crinkled can be hung from expandable rods on selected windows so that privacy is ensured but the lazy summer twilight is allowed to gently filter into the room. The second box can contain small treasures—vases that are less valued and have been collected from many places for an even greater number of years. After the vases, which will soon be filled with flowers of the season, come candles and boxes of potpourri, all scented with your favorite fragrances. The third box can contain more delicate items that can be individually wrapped in layers of fine white tissue. Here can be found a parasol that is practical for hot summer days or just something soft and pretty in front of an empty fireplace. Next come photographs of loved ones that can be taken wherever you go. These are arranged on the tables by which most of your time will be spent—so that you never feel "far" from home.

Your travel boxes may always be filled with dozens of fabrics that range from hardworking cottons to sophisticated linens, to precious lace—all of which can be white.

White is the color of cleanliness and serenity. White is the color of angels, peaceful moonlight, and lily of the valley. It is capable of endless subtleties, is fragile or strong, and can be as transparent as ice or as opaque as marble. It is richly traditional, clean-lined contemporary, rustic country, breezy tropical, and lushly romantic. It is a perfect accent for any room, in any place, at any time.

If the box of linens does not contain enough large pieces for all of the chairs, couches, tables, and footstools, drape individual smaller pieces wherever you choose. Put one on the back of a chair, another on the seat. Such fine fabrics are never too big or too small, too fancy or too plain.

The real beauty of anyplace is often discovered in the natural details and simple grace that comes from abundant bouquets of fresh flowers. They are a nostalgic touch that quiet the soul and scent the air with a sweet perfume. Choose favorite flowers to summon memories of times past. Do not fret about being able to "arrange" garden flowers once they are cut and brought inside. Simply remove all leaves that will be below the waterline and place them in any container that is available. Combine a variety of each in one container or select all of one kind—it matters not. Whichever you choose will decorate any temporary home in your own natural style.

Each of us has photographs of family and friends that we hold dear. Some are serious, some bring the sound of laughter, some are candid, and some are taken by p r o f e s s i o n a l s . Whichever are your favorite, take them along whenever you travel. It need not be a month-long trip to an exotic location to justify packing them with the essentials of travel. An overnight business trip is made more pleasant and often given a loving reassuring smile when favorite photographs are placed close by.

43

There are objects that bring each of us peace; these comforts from home may be brought along on your travels. Such necessities include not only family photographs, but the china which you may be accustomed to using every day. In this way, you are in company with a cherished piece of home that can be used for sipping tea on rainy days, or simply to add charm to an empty bedside table.

Books covered in vintage fabric jackets bring a quiet night's sleep no matter how many times one may have read them. They are like old friends who tell familiar stories of places you have been before. The table may be arranged as at home—perhaps fresh fruit, flowers, a small oriental rug scrap, a piece of favorite china. This is why no matter where you travel, home can always be where your heart is.

A roomy, slipcovered chair, big enough for plopping one's legs over; a new coffee table draped in vintage lace; a vase of roses from the garden—a bit wilted, a few petals missing—an array of vanilla-scented candles adding a warm glow to a now cozy room, these are the elements of effortless, "shabby chic" decorating. It is a rebellion, if you will, from that which is new and perfect. A decorating style that appreciates and feels more than comfortable with furnishings that are well used and have been handed down from generation to generation—a dilapidated elegance, even though you may be able to afford whatever is new that you choose.

It is this—all of this—that may help you feel as though you are home, regardless of where you travel. It is why taking three additional boxes along can be viewed as essential and really not a burden. It is a small inconvenience to justify being comfortable and happy. It is well worth the resulting feeling that there is nowhere else you would rather be than home.

Dining Rooms

How dear to this heart are the scenes of my childhood,
When fond recollection presents them to view!
—Samuel Woodworth

Many can recall with vivid fondness year after year of joyous holidays and family celebrations around a long dining table. Equally cherished are memories of quiet talks, gentle lessons, and treasured moments spent in the kitchen. Among these there are memories of baking cookies with a loved one, having tea with friends, or washing dishes after an enjoyable home-cooked meal. So many of the special times of life are spent with family and friends gathered to chat in the kitchen with the cook, or encircling a beautifully dressed dining-room table. These should be warm, nurturing places for guests and hosts alike. Rooms where the practicality of refrigerators, dishwashers, and microwaves is softened and balanced by the graceful touches you would add to any other room.

Any kitchen and dining room can be decorated in much the same way as other rooms in a Victorian-style home. Many layers of linens and lace, china both old and new, slipcovered chairs in luxurious fabrics, charming treasures, and flowers. Who could resist a tempting tea table bedecked by English porcelain, a bouquet of wildflowers, and draped with spring-colored cloths? Guests will desire to linger over tea and share a secret or two. An everyday dinner can be made worthy of the most poised butler; simply bring out the good china, silver, and crystal. There is no need for a holiday or occasion—any day will be a special day when thoughtful touches of love and fond memories have been made. These are times to be cherished, and to be made beautiful.

Drawing on loved traditions, one can always try to set a table as if everyday were a special day. It is not important if guests have come to call—it can simply be a quiet dinner for one, or an intimate dinner for two. Dishes from treasured collections, matching tablecloth and napkins, and the finest silver can be brought out to make an elegant and pleasing table setting. The contrast of the elegance in the vintage pieces with the fringed edges of the handmade napkins appeals to the eye.

To create these table linens, two yards of a favorite toile print were cut into smaller squares for napkins, a larger square was cut for the tablecloth, and threads were pulled from the edges to create the fringe.

51

Throughout a Victorian-style home, a slightly elegant yet nostalgic touch can be seen. Each room is filled with the memoirs of an era that was elegant, and beautiful. Any home can be made more inviting by rediscovering this ageless decorating style. Here, in this dining room, a family heirloom cloth covers the table where dinner is to be served to celebrate a special occasion. The china, the crystal, and the silver are mismatched, bringing together that which is different, yet very much the same.

Each area in any dining room should hold pieces of nostalgia. This dining room is in a rental home which was temporarily redone. Decorative objects were added to a buffet—some of which were found throughout the home and others obtained from antique stores. Of course, as always there are pitchers filled with fresh flowers and lighted candles.

There is also an old teakettle, found in the cellar, so old that it brings to mind a time when water was warmed on wood-burning stoves. It certainly does not have the delicate fine lines of a traditional Victorian teakettle, but it tells of a generation that was good and simple, and helps to tone down the more formal pieces in the room.

This delightful ensemble creates a backdrop where family and friends can sit for a delicious homemade dinner and good conversation.

It is also a delightful surprise when each area in the dining room is changed with the turning of the seasons. A century ago when flower-scented breezes signaled that summer was at the threshold, homeowners set about welcoming the warm days by rolling up carpets, trading heavy draperies for fine lace, and adding tiny birds in their nests to unexpected places that would hold them.

Here in this dining room, the chandelier has been decked with nests and birds just as in olden days. Sprigs of evergreen and twigs have been woven into the tiny nests, to resemble majestic mountains that are perpetually green with pines and firs, and often lined with the last snow of winter. As spring gets closer the pine boughs will be replaced with the green leaves and flowering stems of lilac bushes, and when summer approaches meadow wildflowers will take their place. When fall is in the air the flowers of summer can be removed and replaced with richly colored fall leaves and ripe acorns.

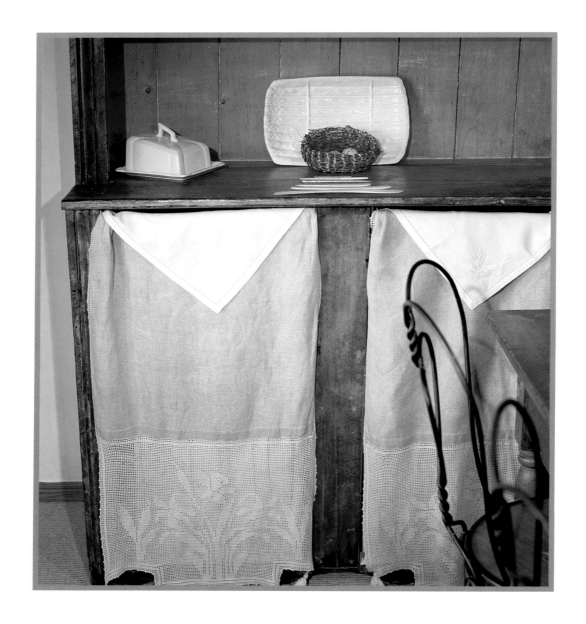

The heart of every home is always in the kitchen. It need not matter whether it is large or small, old or new—it is where everyone wants to be. Even the kitchen linens can be used in very unexpected places. In this kitchen they are draped over the cupboard that stores the family's dishes. It matters not the season when friends return to visit, they are easily tied back so that the vintage dishes can serve the season's fare. Here, an antique cake plate is serving the summer's first fresh berry tart.

And the jocund rebecks sound
To many a youth, and many a maid,
Dancing in the checkered shade.
And young and old come forth to play
On a sunshine holiday.
—John Milton

Dressing a family table in the splendor yet simplicity of the season can be a most pleasing ritual. So for the holiday season, this cupboard's linen doors are opened to gather the red and green dishes for Christmas dinner. This time, the vintage cake plate holds candles to light the evening meal. Red and white antique linens are used for napkins, and small crystal vases with a single red flower are placed where each female guest will be seated. The silver is the best—with pearled handles; but the tiny tumblers are ones that children might select. So as the snow flurries fall and the world becomes quiet, this evening spent by the fire will be inspired by the season, and enjoyed by those who draw on tradition and celebrate in simple homespun luxury.

Whether a home be large or small, a considerable amount of time is spent in the kitchen; so it is very important that each corner be as beautiful as if it were in the center of the room. The view from this kitchen window is not a mountain brook surrounded by wildflowers—it is very near to the side of a neighbors home; but with the window draped in freshly ironed antique linens, held in place by old brass clips and a small collection of ironstone, it is beautiful indeed. In the summer the light filters through the lace and casts a magical shadow on the kitchen table, and in winter one can still see the snow fall and the icicles hanging from the side of the house. It is also attractive to keep favorite teapots and freshly canned preserves out on any kitchen cabinet—it adds a certain hominess; and when friends come to call, everything is close at hand for tea and scones. There is always a pitcher of fresh flowers, for even such a small addition is essential in a room that is so often used and enjoyed by so many.

This is a kitchen with everything in its place, and a place for everything. The old picnic basket on top of the fridge is just waiting for its summer day outside; but during the long days of winter, it is used to store extra linens. The linens on the table and chairs are removed often and replaced with the ones in the basket. On days when one feels like having their own tea party, the table can be dressed in red and white, with blue and white china for contrast, and a much loved dress from childhood can be hung on the back of the door. This is decorating a home in one's own style. A style that can be nostalgic with old-fashioned pinafores, vintage linens, and red table covers—those that are the perfect color for the heart of the home. Nothing else would do in such a special area of this house.

How doth the little busy bee
Improve each shining hour,
And gather honey all the day
From every opening flower!
—Isaac Watts

Not only are the graceful rooms of this home in the mountains filled with flea-market finds that give a look of ageless romance, but so are the porches that greet the guests in the front, and the ones behind the house that are terraced up the side of the mountain. Any summer afternoon, you may find the owner decorating the picnic table with fresh flowers and linens that were made especially for use outdoors. The cloths have boxed corners so that they won't blow around in the canyon breeze; although, the gentle breezes are welcome to caress the lace that hangs from atop the umbrella. Everything that sits upon the tables outside this home has touches of nature. The dishes are those hand-painted with flowers, the creamer is a tiny, white porcelain cow, and the flowers are from the garden. Even the table covers have the colors of the season.

Chic Collectibles

Nothing in the world is single,
All things by a law divine
In one spirit meet and mingle.
—Percy Bysshe Shelley

Most have enjoyed browsing, searching, and shopping flea markets, antique stores, and tiny little shops along forgotten back roads at some time or another. These are the spots where many unique and beloved treasures are found, with which one can fill their home and life. Naturally, each of these lovely finds needs a home, either as a special gift to a loved one, or displayed somewhere in one's own home. As your collections grow, you will begin to love finding new and unexpected ways to weave collectibles in among other objects both old and new, purchased and handmade.

The many different types of china that can be gathered over the years can bring a warm Victorian feeling to any spot, in any room it may be placed. A weathered pine cupboard is filled with the elegance and charm of china, displayed and stacked along with piles of linens. You may fill the cupboard until it overflows, leaving the large doors wide open to display the contents while keeping them at hand for easy use. Place china plates and bowls on shelves inside the window and hang teacups from hooks fastened just below. Any china pitcher may be in use as a flower vase, and serving trays make beautiful places to display other little treasures.

Never worry about the pieces of china you may find being from the same set, or all of your linens and laces matching. You can either place friendly styles and colors together or experiment with playful variety. Let the colors or image in a piece you love inspire you as you fill the entire room. However you use and display your finds, they can always become the heart of any home.

In the early morning hours, the kitchen of this small home is where one can spend time reflecting. It is where one finds the time to do that which they might so enjoy, whether it be stealing a moment of privacy, baking for an evening meal, or arranging dishes and straightening the lace that edges each shelf. It is a time in the quiet of the morning where nothing unwanted intrudes on the soul.

The pine cupboard in the dining room next to the kitchen holds a treasured collection of transferware. In the summer months, next to the dishes can be found the fruits of the garden—a straw hat, fresh tomatoes, even a bouquet of leaves from the apple tree—all of which add an appropriate informality to the formal feeling of vintage lace and Victorian china.

This home is a mirror of Victorian philosophy—all that is important should be, at least in part, gracious, soft, and feminine. Try, with all of the lace and the linens and the old china, to offer a sanctuary in every room—not only for yourself but for all who come to visit. Each tiny space is designed for relaxation and renewal—long talks with cups of herbal tea, quiet afternoons with filtered sun through antique curtains, evenings by the fire for the sharing of dreams since past, and hopes for a future yet to come.

This collection of transferware, with its delicate and fine hand-painted flowers and designs, brings elegance and formality to a simple dining buffet. Every time it is used for a special meal, or gets put away in a new place, it is as if one is seeing it again for the first time. It cannot be explained, but every piece looks so different with each new meal or arrangement.

If you mix the pieces by color and use, they soon paint a picture; if you arrange each collection together by color, they have a story to tell; if you take them by teapot, plate, or cup and saucer and arrange them in a manner of use, they are as the words of a new song. Then place them on glass shelves in a kitchen window, or on top of the buffet in the dining room for yet another delightful change.

What can be enjoyed most about having such a large collection of vintage dishes is how many ways you are able to serve meals made from collected works of much loved recipes. It makes it all the more fun to collect boxes, books, and drawers filled with handwritten recipe cards.

There is a room in many homes that is sometimes a dining room and sometimes a sitting room. It is an intimate place, oftentimes filled with the chatter and laughter of friends or family, and other times with the quiet of intimate conversation. It is a place where nothing seems as if it hadn't always been there, offering serene and familiar security. It is where a weathered wicker chair becomes a stand for the roses that are picked each morning from a garden and where a second wicker chair, not matching of course, is made more comfortable with plump floral pillows that are edged in antique lace.

Matelassé spreads are stacked in the china cupboard; for in the room of a collector, that is exactly where they might be found one moment, and the next somewhere else. A Victorian bust discovered long ago at an eastern antique show sits stately on top of a vintage picnic basket. Upon its head sits a once-worn hat which is one of many that one can "show" whenever and wherever.

All dressed up in winter white with a tiny touch of red—just to remind all how special each and every piece of a collection can be. When one is asked about a certain spread, or an individual dish, or a particular carved candlestick, it can be as if turning through the pages of an old photograph album. With each piece, a collector can almost always remember where they were, who they were with, and the history they were told when they purchased the item. It is good to know the information about each piece that you collect, so that when they are given away or sold, the recipient can understand the history and the value of each newly acquired treasure. Not having information is like a photograph with no names, and no brief stories of when and where it was taken.

We may affirm absolutely that nothing great
in the world has been accomplished without passion.
—Georg Wilhelm Friedrich Hoegel

When private collections are being discussed, it never ceases to surprise one the great value that is attached to certain items by owners or appraisers. It is true that some pieces hold an intrinsic value due to their age or previous owner, but even those estimates seem arbitrary. In some instances just because it is old doesn't mean it should be valuable—it may not have been a nice piece when it was new! There is more of a value in an old linen dishtowel that your grandmother embroidered when she was sixteen than one of a thousand tablecloths owned by royalty. You should buy and treasure your collections—not for a value assigned by someone else—but for what they mean to you. They need not be in perfect condition, they need not be made of expensive materials, they need not be highly sought after—they need only mean something.

Different tables, different treasure chests of china, different laces and linens—even with the same passions, the same likes, the same dislikes, all that is owned and purchased by collectors of Victorian pieces is so very different. These can usually be found among friends who share the same passion for living around the elegance of this Victorian-chic style. In this manner, being a small part of someone else's passion offers you twice the vision for decorating your home. A true collector gives ideas and notions, and adopts many from others for their own style as well.

Sometimes collections begin and even the collector is surprised. The pieces laid before you are not pieces most Victorian decorators would usually collect—they don't resemble anything Victorian—but for reasons that ring a chord in the heart, they can be among one's most cherished. These rustic wooden kitchen tools are not items that would normally appeal to one who loves vintage linens, delicate lace, and fragile dinnerware. However, their purity of form and their simplicity of materials may appeal to you. The stories they could tell of families gathered together making dinner, mothers baking for the holidays, or children helping to prepare for a family celebration, are pages of which one may want to be a part. It is true that, "it is only with the heart that one can see rightly; what is essential is invisible to the eye."

Christmas Splendor

Yes, . . . there is a Santa Claus. . . . Thank God! he lives, and he lives forever. A thousand years from now, . . . nay ten times ten thousand years from now, he will continue to make glad the heart of childhood!

—Francis Pharcellus Church

For so many people, the winter holidays are the most treasured times of the year. What a marvelous reason to pull out all the best ribbons and lace, baubles and bears. Every moment of the season is loved; from the first frost-covered morning that whispers "it's time to begin the festive preparations," to the winter's first fire-lit evening, when precious ornaments are unwrapped from their clean, white tissue paper. Outside, the jubilant voices of warmly bundled carolers spark the imagination with visions of Victorian carolers of years ago. Thank them for their songs of cheer with offerings of hot chocolate and cider touched with cinnamon. Then there is the joy of making and writing Christmas cards filled with messages of hopes and dreams for family and friends.

For Christmas, you can fill your home with the scents, tastes, and visions of both the Christmases of your youth and the splendor of Victorian Christmases past, filled with sentiment and anticipation. Drape fragrant pine boughs from shelves and doorways. Make wreaths of wonderful odds and ends such as ribbons, buttons, tiny dolls, or dried fruit. The Christmas tree can be decked with silver stars, sugarplums, candles, cherubs, nesting birds, and anything else that is loved.

The Victorian Christmas was a family affair, as it is for many today. The chatter, laughter, and thank you's as gifts that are exchanged remind one of those olden days when aunts and uncles and close family friends shared their joyous celebrations for the holiday season.

When the first snow frosts the rooftops, you may begin to focus your attention to the detail of decorating for the holidays by gathering old quilts and tasseled trim, linen, velvet, and toile. Scent the air with candied orange peel, and fill the house with the harmonies of Christmas music. It is these glimpses of the past that make an ideal setting for a traditional Christmas to delight your holiday visitors.

With colors of faded greens and creams—the very palette of winter—dress your home for the coming days of celebration. A new cover for the chair, but old lace to make it feel at home, ornaments from Christmases past, dolls made for grandchildren, and stockings hung in the most unexpected of places are only a few of the special details meant to delight our holiday guests.

With Christmas boughs amid the china pitchers atop a well-worn hutch, ornaments hanging from any-place, linen and lace covering tables and chairs, and the table always set for Christmas tea, one may spend hour upon hour decorating the home like the pages from a storybook that might be given as a gift on Christmas eve. Many may ask why, and a truth-ful reply might be, "because it is a warm and welcome setting for a holi-day celebration, which is one of the best gifts that can be given to family and friends."

Take great delight in gather-ing all that you love from the tradi-tions of years since past and using them to create personal and family traditions for years yet to come. Lavish both old and new ornaments upon the tree, handmade gifts can be carefully selected and made for those you love, and parties are planned for when the December snows fall quiet-ly around you. It is a time for the giv-ing and the sharing of the simple gifts of Christmas.

One of the true joys of the holiday season is to travel to the homes of family and friends. In the crisp evening air of winter, you may find yourself bundled up as you make your way from one celebration to the next, enjoying all of the wonderments of the holidays.

A home may decorated with the simplicity and love of America's earlier days. A kitchen table can be set with a nineteenth-century heritage, and the air can be filled with the wonderful scents of oranges, cloves, holly berries, and evergreen. Everywhere you look are the collections of dolls and teddy bears. Some may have been lovingly created, and others received as gifts from loved ones. Whenever you enter a home like this, you may look at Christmas as if through the eyes of a child and see only magic.

It may feel just as exciting to enter a friend's drawing room, filled with vintage toys and dolls, as when you peered into the shop windows at Christmas when you were young. The faces of the dolls and the teddy bears that sit quietly beneath the trees are like the faces of loved ones. Each, dressed in holiday finery, has a twinkle in her eye and a secret in her heart—and when one listens carefully, one can hear their stories of Christmases past.

Whenever a dear friend is visited during the season, you may also find their rooms aglow with candlelight, unexpected scents, and good cheer. The fireplace here is not a real one, but the mantle and hearth are trimmed in fresh pine branches and lavished with lights and ornaments. It is as warm to all who gather round as if it were ablaze with a yuletide log. Every room in a home can be filled with the scents of the foods that are sometimes traditional, and sometimes not, at Christmas. It is a gathering place for family and friends to delight in all of nature's bounty, and to reflect on the sentiment that this season of seasons always has to offer.

Heap on more wood!—the wind is chill;
But let it whistle as it will,
We'll keep our Christmas merry still.
—Sir Walter Scott

In this home, there are several smaller trees throughout, and this feather tree in the bedroom is delightfully decorated with tiny ornaments that have been handmade. One might be more accustomed to the cooking that is so expected at this time of year, than to the sewing of little beads and buttons or lace to these heart-shaped pillows. However, the detail on each ornament is not too difficult, and shows off the imagination and attention to the finer points that add tiny unexpected touches to everything.

It is the charm of the little things that brings comfort into the home, and the holiday season is an ideal setting for as many small touches as you desire. Brighten any small place with tiny votive candles, hang miniature ornaments all around your home, or place cinnamon-scented pinecones in a basket near your door to create an undertone of holiday cheer that every guest will be sure to feel.

There are not very many rich-colored velvets or iridescent silks in this home for the holidays—only the echoes of laughter and simplicity of holidays past. To make a house a home, one can be an avid collector of Victorian recipes as well as smaller touches that are completely Victorian, such as hand-embroidered doilies, lace tablecloths, and individual ornaments that hang from a living-room tree. Each is selected carefully and placed with the deliberate intent of making them very much a part of this comfortable room. As winter's pale daylight fades and the delicate, splendid sight of icicles shimmers through each room as they cling to frosted windowpanes, the guests who visit here will feel the spirit of Christmas that will bless them, one and all.

Bedroom Comfort

If there is a paradise on the
face of the earth,
It is this, oh! it is this, oh! it is this.
—Anonymous

Of all the rooms in one's home, the bedroom is the most relaxing, the place in which one may feel the most tranquil. To create this feeling, you can begin decorating it in soothing shades of white. There can be fresh eyelet sheets and pillowcases, the gentle texture of a white lace or matelassé coverlet, and a soft wash of creamy white on the walls. Restful colors are brought into play in a variety of ways—wonderfully embellished pillows for the bed or chair, an added blanket of gentle pink, or dream-filled pastel prints on the walls and nightstand. This abundance of white with soft colors not only calms and quiets, it allows the eyes to rest upon the simple but exquisite details in the room. Lacy curtains also bring a comforting, yet elegant look to any bedroom, whether dark and rich, or cool and white. Close by can

be a spot of color in a sea of clouds—a painted tray holding a gathering of seashells, or an armful of daffodils in a china pitcher near the bed. The mountains of pillows that can be collected from all over, or stitched together from scraps of lovely fabric, are so inviting and luxurious that you might often wish to lounge there all day. Since you must eventually leave your soft haven, you can add a warm rug near the side of the bed for bare feet to find on chilly mornings. At your bedside could be a table for a quaint lamp with a lacy shade or a plentitude of candles for soft, gentle light by which to write the day's thoughts before drifting to sleep.

For all of your moments, both waking and sleeping, your bedroom should be your most restful and romantic refuge, a place that truly reflects your dreams.

A tiny bit of traditional wisdom: a cut of lemon, a splash of rose water, starched white linens, an expected abundance of lace pillows, and soft lights that inspire one to whisper are what will make a bedroom a place where dreams are guests—a quiet place for listening to no one's thoughts but your own, or a luxurious retreat for two.

The bedroom is no longer just a place for sleeping, but a place of refuge and an oasis of comfort where we retreat to read, sip a cup of tea, or share the stories of the day. Bedrooms are such personal spaces, so they should be designed and decorated with particular and individual care. This is not a room to give to a decorator, but a room to surround whoever visits here with all that is familiar and restful.

That which comes to mind with these three statements is different to each of us. To some it is layers of linens and lace, antique wicker furniture, vintage sleepwear from exotic places, down-filled pillows, and matelassé coverlets. To another it might be a gracefully curved sleigh bed with plaid flannel sheets, a braided rug on a wooden floor, and candles that scent the air with pine and woodland flowers. It matters not what it is, only that it's what you want it to be. You will rest more completely when all your needs are attended to and all of your senses are soothed.

You may sleep more soundly and awake more refreshed with cool breezes to calm you at night, and natural light to wake you gently in the morning. This bed was placed beneath an eastern window so that the early sun could filter through the lace curtains, and the evening breeze could gently blow the vintage panels through the painted French doors.

A thing of beauty is a joy forever:
Its loveliness increases; it will never
Pass into nothingness; but still will keep
A bower quiet for us, and a sleep
Full of sweet dreams, and health, and quiet breathing.
—John Keats

Often, it is the small nooks and corners—places to read, think, or work in peace—that nurture sweet dreams or daydreams. These are the places that can simply and quietly make a bedroom special.

A tiny table tucked in a corner covered with layers of a grandmother's lace holds a single candle, copies of favorite books, and a private journal. It is here that one can snuggle in at night with artwork that inspires, fresh flowers that linger with the scents of summer, and personal treasures. This is where one may choose to end each day, but another favorite place to begin each day may be a writing desk in a different corner, nestled beside a window. It is here that one can go each morning with a cup of tea to catch up on correspondence. These are the places that rest a weary body and enlighten the mind.

The bed—whether a sleigh style, canopy, pencil post, or rustic cast-iron—is inevitably the visual focus of the bedroom, but coverings and comfort are what make it inviting. The necessities of any bed are a headboard tall enough for leaning against while reading, a frame that has no sharp edges, and a deep mattress chosen for its balance of support and softness. Bed linens of natural fibers that wear well with age and repeated washings, and breath to keep you cool in the summer and warm during winter, are also much needed. The luxurious nonessential amenities are layers of linens and lace, antique quilts, vintage down pillows made from the chintz pinafores from childhood, and a place for serving and enjoying tea. All of these are that which add a humble quiet grace to a hectic modern life.

A love of aged things can benefit not only one's individual need to be surrounded by that which has a history, but conservation and the environment as well. When second-hand furnishings and flea-market finds are repaired or repainted, or simply enjoyed as is, there is less "stuff" being made and fewer resources being used. The sun-softened colors and worn texture in vintage natural wood furniture give a richness that only deepens with use.

Just as quilts often tell a visual family history with pieces cut from childhood dresses or scraps rescued from a great-aunt's sewing box, so can curtains, pillows, shams, and tea cozies be fashioned from pieces of vintage fabric and finished with antique laces and trims. Collections such as these make a room more personal and comfortable. All the better if they are objects with a job to do—such as quilts to warm you through the coldest months of winter.

Many yearn for a simpler life—based on quiet, and comfort, and pleasures rather than possessions—guided by uncomplicated needs rather than trends. Here in the fresh uncluttered style of the these two bedrooms, one finds a pared-down, earth-friendly retreat. The decorations are minimal and those that are used are borrowed from nature, or collected from places once visited or families who no longer found a use for them.

Bedrooms enriched with predominant shades of white and cream, bold accents of color, the texture of bare wood, natural flooring, and weathered metals have an appeal that is obvious—the effects of such rooms are calming and relaxing, the decorations and soft furnishings are a combination of old and new, and the look is timeless. In addition, the practicality of such a room is a key element—these, after all, are rooms that are meant to be lived in, not simply looked at. Their simplicity of style with an emphasis on natural, once-used materials is still and forever fresh. It has, after all, been subjected to, and passed the test of time.

Love comforteth like sunshine after rain.
—William Shakespeare

Those who are collectors, and therefore naturally love an overabundance of anything, find comfort in a bedroom that has more than the absolute basics and down-to-earth functionality. For some it is about including meters of swagged lace, soft furnishings, plump beds and pillows, mismatched color combinations, and extravagant ornamentation and accessories. After all, cushions piled high on a bed seem to soften the entire room. Don't ever feel compelled to use the same matching fabrics for all of the cushions and coverlets. By varying the texture, style, pattern, and color, a room has more to say. After the furnishings are complete, come the fine details that can make a room so personal. Gather together favorites that have been collected over the years and display them on small nightstands or occasional tables placed out of the way but somewhere in the room. This will surely add personality to your room.

The bath, more than any room in the house, should be a haven of soothing sanctuary. Old wood and vintage brass fixtures, and a deep porcelain bathtub—one that lets you lie back and soak in water up to your neck—create an atmosphere of cleanliness and calm, with no "modern" distractions.

When guests enter to freshen up, think how delighted they would be to find layers of lace draped over the side of the tub and flowers placed neatly in the bottom. One could hold an exquisite party, and surprise their guests by filling an antique bathtub with water and then placing an abundance of water lilies and floating candles inside. When guests enter throughout the evening hours you might hear cries of sheer delight.

Scent is an element in decorating that cannot be seen, but is as important in establishing a mood and a feeling of comfort as any visible accessory in the room.

It is an especially enjoyable and relatively inexpensive way to enhance the pleasures of the bedroom and the bath. Honeysuckle vines growing outside the window will add fragrance to the breeze. A bath sachet of chamomile, a vase of fresh flowers on the nightstand, a tiny sachet of lavender placed under the coverlets, or a sleep pillow of balsam needles add the sensory riches of nature to an evening of pampering and relaxation.

When the flowers in the garden begin to fade, the rose petals can be saved to scent a dresser drawer, mint leaves can be tossed into the bath; and one can even iron linens with lavender water that is made at home. Scent is so very important because the bed and bath are places to indulge all the senses, to create a haven in which one can feel fully rested and relaxed, and find comfort and peace at the end of the day.

The same neutral palette in these two rooms has two entirely different interpretations. In this room the colors help to illustrate a romantic tale. One that begins with window coverings that are, in reality, vintage wedding gowns, and layers of beautifully made pillows whose fabrics and trims have stories of their own to tell.

In the room on the facing page, a rendering of pure natural country is painted. There are no ruffles and lace here, only simple lines with a hint of feminine accents—a clean, and much less fussy style.

After restoring an older home, one that might even be considered vintage, where authentic and natural are words used often in relation to the decor, beds can again wear their wrinkles and their tiny tears proudly. A bed dressed in the soft shades of unbleached cotton or fine white linen can look just as beautiful as, and feel more restful than, a bed screaming for attention in bright floral or funky patterns. In the same manner, vintage linens, of which include soft pillowcases made of homespun ticking or antique lace, hand-sewn sheets, mismatched draperies, and hand-pieced quilts, can all bring a humble grace to a once old and deserted room.

Over the years, one might find that not only have they come to rely on the basics in their home, but that which is considered by some to be the frivolities as well. The big old bed upon which one not only sleeps but shares secrets and dreams, the nightstand that often holds a favorite children's book or a serving for tea, the hat rack immediately outside the door that hasn't held a hat for years but gently holds pieces of lace that one has yet to decide what shall be made of them—these are the basics and these are important, but what surrounds them are just as necessary to make the picture complete. The collections and memorabilia that you own change and evolve as your life changes and evolves, but it is the unmistakable pleasure of collecting, displaying, rearranging, and remaking each one that offers comfort and joy to each new day of life.

With the simple white walls and the old pine floors in this bedroom, you can take those basics that are essential, scatter, layer, and wrap important nonessentials around them, on them, or under them, and make each look as fancy or as plain as you feel. Each room, when newly decorated, suggests a way of life that once was simpler, more gentile, more beautiful somehow. In rooms such as these, you can smell the fragrances from the garden as the breeze blows them gently through the windows, you can see the patterns of light that filter through the sheer lace curtains, and you can almost hear the slap of the screen door in the summertime as friends come to call—this is the way it should be.

Victorian Outdoors

All that in this delightful garden grows,
Should happy be, and have immortal bliss.
—Edmund Spenser

The enchanted cottages of many a childhood imagination may have all had one thing in common, a bright and fragrant trellised porch. The outside may oftentimes be a favorite place to be. Just as nature can be brought indoors with fresh flowers and sunlit rooms, you can also create beautiful garden rooms outdoors. Nature happily provides most of the art and light you will need. To these, you can add a few graceful "indoor" touches to make a lovely outdoor corner as comfortable as any living room.

Outside, find new spots for wicker furniture, which moves effortlessly from sitting room to veranda. Plump up wicker chairs with soft cushions in pretty floral prints. Top a well-aged and weathered table with a lacy white tablecloth and an assortment of favorite things, all arranged for an afternoon's refreshment or teatime snack. You will never need a reason for a joyful picnic. The welcoming trees and flowers all dressed in their finery offer infinite cause for celebration. These, combined with the elegance of fine china and lace, are reminiscent of a more relaxed time. A time when people lingered over tea and talk, and gathered often over natural carpets of green for picnics and parties. A time when parasols or lacy umbrellas sheltered fair skin from summer sun.

Outdoors you can freely play with whimsical touches and fanciful figures right out of a fairy tale or enchanted cottages from your youth. It matters not from where you draw your inspiration, as long as it is yours.

A sun-filled breakfast room, an inviting screened-in porch, a charming potting shed, a rose-covered gazebo—these are all examples of a Victorian outdoor "garden room," designed with the simple pleasures of life in mind. Regardless of their size, shape, or location, areas in the garden are all spaces of delight. Here, one can entertain family, talk away the hours with friends, or sit quietly alone, all the while surrounded by the sights, scents, and sounds of the garden.

It is spaces like these—within the garden—that the passions of the gardener, collector, and decorator are all reflected. They are places filled with very comfortable furniture; striking combinations of color, style, and texture; and cherished collections of family treasures—all along side a stunning array of fresh flowers and amid the sounds of the birds as they sing from the trees.

In the summer months, the garden is always right there, beautiful and inviting. It can be a place of casual charm, one of disciplined beauty, or one of natural abundance. It can be a center for entertaining or a quiet place for a romantic gathering. It can be a "room" outside that is as important as any room inside. It can be where the love of gardening actually transcends the need for organized flower beds or preplanned vegetable patches. This is a very special place that, for most, can be enjoyed only during certain months of the year. It is not like the kitchen that one can enter and sit for awhile any day of any month of any year. It is not a place that one can easily leave unattended, knowing it will be the same on return.

Outdoor barbecues, picnics for holidays, simple lunches on the patio, and brides who plan the most important day of their lives—for all, there is the desired hope, kindness, and understanding of mother nature. There should be no rain, no wind, no blazing afternoon sun. All must be just right—which is why the time enjoyed is so memorable and so favored. It is a place where one can steal moments of the day or hours of the evening on very splendid days.

A noise like of a hidden brook
In the leafy month of June,
That to the sleeping woods all night
Singeth a quiet tune.
—Samuel Taylor Coleridge

When lunch is served in the garden it need not be a five-course meal, beginning with appetizers and ending with flaming desserts, to be a grand affair. Linen and lace tablecloths, vintage baskets filled with aged cheese and fine wines, home-baked bread and brandied preserves, fresh flowers in crystal glasses— it is as delicious and as memorable as lunch served at high noon at Sardi's.

The atmosphere in such a setting, depending on the intensity of the sun, the clouds overhead, and the wafting of warm breezes, ranges from sublime to romantic, to euphoric. Like any place that has known such great happiness, nostalgia pervades a garden in a home where family and friends have gathered for special occasions—or no occasion at all. For now and for a long time to come, families will gather here, friends will meet here, and they will find peace here.

Off the back of this house sits a series of terraced porches that were accidentally designed for both practical purposes and entertaining possibilities. From each private section, one can see the view of the majestic rocky mountains, smell the wildflowers that grow everywhere along the hills, and hear the musical sounds of the birds and the animals. It is a place that is almost always set for an afternoon of casual chatter, for a ladies luncheon, or for dining by candlelight on a summer night as the hours are talked away. One can enjoy this quiet space every morning as the sun peeks over the mountains and helps to welcome a day that is filled with happiness and harmony.

What is a weed?
A plant whose virtues
have not yet been discovered.
—Ralph Waldo Emerson

Antique and garden purists may surround themselves with nothing but authentic garden furnishings and tools from one particular period or style. However, most collectors do not have that luxury—or desire. In some ways, an eclectic collection for the outdoors, borrowing freely from many periods and styles, has a more lasting interest. A one-note collection can wear thin. When eclectic collections have a common thread—decorating for the garden plus the taste of the collector—they give any space a unique and decorative stamp.

Decorating for the garden is, in actuality, as much fun for many as decorating for a home. The porches are an extension of the home, and are similar to open garden rooms. The sitting porch has a friendly cluttered air, while the dining porch is more sparse and more functional. Place various pieces on the porches surrounding a home, and you will see they often have a dramatic end result. When the midafternoon sun is shining one can sit amidst cups and teapots adorned in floral prints, and be charmed by the way they look against the backdrop of a cloudless blue sky with the sun sparkling through the leaves on the trees, and the breeze carrying scents from the garden. These are better than those offered by any scented candle indoors.

When one lives in the mountains, they usually love the changing of the seasons; but it is always a little saddening to most when the brisk winds of fall begin to blow and the garden furnishings need to come inside for the months of winter. Bring wicker furniture inside to help brighten those shorter darker days—a task that indicates a change is in the air.

You might always be just a little surprised, while scouring flea markets and garage sales, when you see that someone has thrown away pieces of old wicker furniture. No matter how tattered and torn, they can still be used for so many wonderful things. Here is one picked up for pennies that acts as a plant stand for geraniums. It is more charming than a new stand that has no history or character.

That which is old and considered by some to no longer be worthy of a place in their homes is re-used here as a decorative theme for this garden. Such weathered pieces as these can oftentimes be found at rummage, and yard sales. Many broken tools, unraveled baskets, and ripped quilts have been tossed into a pile to be given or thrown away, but these are those accents and accessories with character, which have endured many afternoons of hot dessert sun and many cold snow-covered nights.

Have you ever noticed how "unrealistic" a new piece can look when placed in your garden? Paint that has not chipped, wood that has not cracked, finishes that have not faded simply do not belong in a garden that is created by collectors and antiquers. Such gardens can be filled with memories of summers spent long ago.

A much loved section in this garden is pictured on the right. All that has been collected here is truly cherished. If you look very closely, you can see that the tiers are edged, not with traditional terra-cotta tiles, but rather with plates from a collection. These plates are some whose patterns were not favored, most of which were purchased for only pennies; so it matters not that they might chip or break in the garden. The cherub-supported birdbath has been adorned with shells that have been collected on a visit to the sea. White seashells rim the concrete basin, and a mosaic flowerpot with shells is turned upside down in the middle of the bath to act as a perch for any feathered visitor who might stop for a quiet moment and a cool drink. There is an old scale that often acts as a plant stand, and old tin pots that hold this season's flowering plants.

This potting table, used often during the months from spring until fall, was purchased at a rummage sale. It doesn't have wooden doors to keep the tools safely inside, but instead, it has lace curtains to bring a little of the inside out. They are held with clothespins on a clothesline for easy drying and easy removal. The drapes may be changed to match the color of the flowers on top. Change these pieces on the outside of your home as often as you might those on the inside.

Where the house meets the garden, there lies romantic potential—be it a glorious view, a shady terrace, a field of wildflowers, or a flower-filled conservatory—for it is the beauty, the color, and the fragrance of flowers that creates a feast for all of the senses. None more so than those from an English country garden, which have an innocence and freshness all their own. Armfuls of pink night-scented stocks, honeysuckle, and patches of spearmint and wintergreen will fill the air with a nostalgic mixture of summery scents and will delight the eye with a palette of soft rain-washed colors. What better place to walk, to have quiet conversations, to wonder, to plan, to dream, to remember?

Index